Welcome

Welcome to the start of a wonderful journey. When you reach the end of this book you will have discovered a new set of skills to practice and you will be on your way towards delivering presentations with impact and ease.

Presenting Without Fear

Derek E Fox

DF-Leap

www.DFLeap.com
info@dfleap.com
© 2010 DF-Leap

All images provided by Graham Ogilvie

http://www.ogilviedesign.co.uk/

Content:

For Denise and Charlie, thank you for supporting me.

The gift you give me is the joy I see in your smile every day.

Chapter one: About Presentations

Destroying the myths behind presentations

1

About Presentations

If we actually believed everything we read about presentations no one would ever present again.

There have been many books and articles written on presentation skills over the years. While most are very good and informative, some are full of myths and false truths. These myths and false truths have only served to increase the stress and discomfort associated with public speaking and presentations.

This short chapter will look at the most common myths about presentations and prove each one wrong, or expose it for the false exaggeration it actually is. There is no secret skill, or special trait people are born with which is required for professional presentations. It is a combination of preparation, practice, and perfecting a set of simple techniques that will help to deliver presentations with impact and ease.

Myth

'Great presenters are born, no one can develop this talent'

Fact:

Even accomplished speakers have to start at the beginning, developing their skills, controlling their nerves, and trying to overcome the fear of public speaking. If you need evidence take a look at Bill Clinton (acknowledged as a professional speaker) on the internet delivering some of his early career speeches and enjoy.

No one is born with the talent for public speaking; it is a skill that can be developed. Think back to a time when you had to learn a new skill, maybe it was cycling a bicycle, reading and writing, or driving a car. Remember the first time you attempted this new skill? How easy was that? Take driving for example, the first time you sat behind the wheel and had to take control. The experience was nerve wreaking, the car was in control, you felt uncomfortable, nervous, and wished it was over. Did that first experience stop you from trying again? When your need is greater than your fear you find the strength and courage to try again, and again, until finally you master the challenge.

Today you may find yourself driving without fear, you are in control, driving is simply something you do to get from one place to another. How did you achieve this? You developed the skills, from the initial fear and discomfort you practiced and developed the required competence. As your competence grew so did your confidence, until finally you mastered the skills required. The same learning cycle can be applied to presentations. To master the skills and overcome the fear you simply have to practice and develop the skills required.

Myth

'I am an introvert, presentations are for extroverts'

Fact:

Some of the world's greatest public speakers have a preference for introversion: Ghandi, Martin Luther King, Mary Robinson, and Nelson Mandela are just a few examples. In fact some of the greatest screen actors also have a preference for introversion, yet they deliver commanding performances full of passion and emotion.

Introversion can be explained as your preference of how you draw energy. According to Carl Jung (Swiss psychologist whose work led to the Myers Briggs type indicator, or MBTI tool) a person with a preference for introversion draws their energy from their internal world, like a battery powered appliance. They enjoy reflection, and deep thinking. They expend additional energy when they have to think on their feet, engaging at length with large groups, and react to situations without having the time to reflect. A person with a preference for extroversion draws their energy from the external work, like a solar powered appliance. They enjoy engaging with large groups, reacting to situations without reflection, and thinking on their feet. What drains their energy is having to reflect deeply, or disengage from the external work to reflect.

Introversion and extroversion are our preference to where we draw energy. It is true that presentations will draw less energy from a person with a preference for extroversion; however, this same person will be exhausted planning for their presentation. The person with a preference for introversion will expend more energy while presenting, however, they will enjoy the planning more. So having a preference for introversion will help your presentations through the planning phase.

Myth

'I am no good with all that technology stuff"

Fact

Presentations are about YOU the presenter; you do not need technology to deliver a presentation. Using technology may take away from your presentation if people only remember the great graphics and not the message you delivered. Martin Luther King did not have any flashy technology when he delivered his memorable speech. You are the presenter everything else is just a presentation aid. Think back to some of the most memorable speeches or presentations in history, can you remember the technology used? Very few great presentations rely on technology to deliver the message; it is simply a way to enhance a strong well-structured message delivered by a great presenter.

Technology is a wonderful thing, if used in the right situations. As a presenter you should focus on the message of your presentation and the structure of delivery. Once you master these elements of presentation you can then look at ways to enhance the delivery through using visual or auditory aids. There are plenty of simple to use tools available today that can enhance your presentation through visual and auditory aids. Later in this book we will look at delivery skills and how to use technology to aid your presentation.

Technology is not something to be feared. If you would like to use technology to enhance your presentation then look at what you need and learn how to use it. Also have a back-up plan, remember the presentation is about you not the technology. If you turn up to a venue and find the technology is not available or is not functioning correctly, then you can still deliver your great presentation on a flip chart or in a discussion.

Myth

'I don't have the voice for presentations'

Fact

Everyone can develop a good presentation voice. It is simply a matter of **S**peed, **T**one, **E**motion, **P**rojection, and the effective use of **S**ilence. These STEPS are easily developed through simple training methods such as reading a children's fairy tale, or playing the characters from your favourite film. You do not need to be the next soprano or have the depth of a blues singer, for presentations you need a clear well-paced voice that moves with your presentation and projects emotions and clarity to your audience.

For people who are interested here is a basic overview of how your voice works. The human voice consists of sound made   by using the vocal folds (cords) for talking, singing, laughing, screaming, etc. Generally speaking, the mechanism for generating the human voice can be subdivided into three parts; the lungs, the vocal folds within the larynx, and the articulators. The lung must produce adequate airflow and air pressure to vibrate vocal folds (this air pressure is the fuel of the voice). The vocal folds are a vibrating valve that chops up the airflow from the lungs into audible pulses that form the laryngeal sound source. The muscles of the larynx adjust the length and tension of the vocal folds to 'fine tune' pitch and tone. The articulators above the larynx consisting of: the tongue, palate, cheek, lips, etc. articulate and filter the sound emanating from the larynx and to some degree can interact with the laryngeal airflow to strengthen it or weaken it as a sound source.

Reading stories, singing, or playing characters from a film will develop and strengthen the muscles required to develop your presentation voice.

Myth

'I always forget everything I am going to say'

Fact

The human brain can only focus on 5-9 items at a time. If you are managing your nerves, worrying about your performance, or thinking about the questions the audience are going to ask this will leave little space for the information you want to retain. Thankfully there are several easy ways to remember all of the information you want to present. From practice to visual road-maps these simple techniques will allow you to recall all the information you require in your presentation.

There are many memory improvement books on the market, different techniques work for different people. Some enjoy mind mapping, while others find association works best for them. Find the right technique that suits your style the best. While you are exploring these ranges of techniques you can also use the following generic methods to help increase memory recall. Use visual aids as a road-map, key images or pictures that will trigger your memories. Have numbers such as dates, statistics, times, etc. documented on key slides, posters, or flip charts. If you are using a flip chart remember you can always write information in a light pencil beforehand (the audience cannot see this), and fill it in during the presentation. A poster at the back of the room with your key information also helps as it will be within your view but out of the audiences view. Practice, practice, practice, there is no substitution for a well-rehearsed performance.

Find the technique that suits you best and use it. Remember to always use aids in recall. Making things memorable will be covered later in the book.

Myth

'I will die if they ask me a question I cannot answer'

Fact

People are inquisitive by nature, so most people will always ask questions. This shows they are listening and are interested in your presentation. For questions you cannot answer that is okay, it is how you tell the audience you do not know that is the key. Standing dumbfounded and wide-eyed while fumbling for an answer is not the best way to handle a tough question. Instead, acknowledge the question, explain you do not have the answer on hand but commit to how and when you will have the answer for the person who asked.

Bridging is a technique used by professional presenters where they 'bridge' from the question to the answer. This bridge may be an acknowledgement, *'That's a great question'* or ' *It is interesting you asked that question as...*' Asking is another bridging technique, here you simply ask for more information to clarify the question, *'In what way do you mean'* or *'Do you mean locally or globally'*. A more advanced (and sometimes tricky) bridge is the adapt technique. The adapt technique requires the presenter to pick up on key words within the question, and reference these words while giving the answer you want the audience to hear. A word of caution here, this technique takes practice, if used incorrectly it will appear you are just 'dodging the question'.

A bridge allows you time to gather your thoughts and formulate your answer. Later in the book we will explore four simple techniques for dealing with questions. Good preparation will also allow you to think about what difficult questions may be asked and how to answer them.

Myth

'I am not good with people, they will not like me'

Fact

Most audience members are just as nervous as the presenter. They may be worried you are going to ask them questions, or make them uncomfortable by doing something they may dislike. Audience members want your presentation to go well, they are mostly there to support and encourage you. There are a range of simple techniques for building rapport and connection with the audience, but none are simpler than just being yourself. They know you and are comfortable with you.

There are a lot of 'tricks' to help people like you such as giving them a gift, free tea/coffee, making a joke about yourself, or simply connecting with them on a common issue *'can you believe what Tom said yesterday!'* A very easy technique to build rapport is 'liking'. The more you can be 'just **like** them' the more they will **like** you. Dress similar, use the same language, and refer to common examples. Share their hopes and concerns. There are advanced rapport techniques such as voice commands and body language matching, and these will be discussed later in the book, for now feel good that even if it does not seem like it the audience are there to support you.

It is possible that some audience members want to *'hijack'* your presentation as they may have an alternative motive or an *'axe to grind'* with you. Dealing with difficult participants is just another skill you can develop. Later in the book we will explore 'psychological judo' a technique designed to disarm 'hecklers' and build your credibility with the audience members.

Myth

'Presentations are a performance, I am not a performer'

Fact

Presentations are about YOU the presenter delivering your information, selling your ideas, or influencing people towards a decision. The most important part of the presentation is the outcome, what do you want the audience members thinking, feeling, or doing at the end of your presentation?

Most people want to be entertained, however, not at the cost of the content. A great performance is only respected when the content of the performance is also excellent. By practicing a range of simple techniques provided in this book you will develop the skills to deliver memorable presentations that deliver results. Along the way you will also pick up tips and tricks on how to 'polish' your presentation and deliver a performance that not only leaves the audience feeling good, but also delivers the outcome you want from the presentation. A presenter that just jumps around the room banging flip charts will not win over many audiences, remember, people are there to listen to your presentation. They want substance, not performance. When you deliver substance WITH an appropriate performance this enhances the positive experience of the audience members and they walk away with your memorable presentation firmly imbedded in their minds, ready to take action.

Above all you are the presentation, the message you deliver and the experience you give the audience is key to achieving the outcomes you desire. Developing skills that enhances the transfer of the message will serve to increase the positive experience for the audience members.

These are but a few of the common myths that surround presenting and public speaking. As you have seen these myths are based on false evidence or exaggerated facts. Throughout this book you will be introduced to simple techniques and easy to apply methods for delivering memorable presentations. From dealing with fear to polishing your delivery we will explore the skills required to master presenting without fear.

There are many forms of presenting including:

- Sales presentations
- Information sharing
- Public speaking
- Speeches
- Presenting awards
- Presenting facts/figures
- Meetings
- Reports
- Training

The techniques covered in this book can be applied to all the presentation situations you may be faced with. From one-on-one discussions to large presentations in an auditorium, the underlying fundamentals are the same: controlling your nerves, preparation, structure, and delivery. Each area will be dealt with in turn. You will discover simple techniques and explore a range of tips and tricks used by the professionals to help enhance your presentation skills. Step by step you will build your confidence and competence towards mastering the skill of presenting without fear.

Just imagine the successful feelings you will experience once you have the ability to deliver with impact. You have started a journey towards excellence, now it is time to continue developing your success.

By removing the barrier of myths and misunderstanding you have taken the first step towards presenting without fear. Soon you will have developed the skills to deliver memorable presentations with impact.

Chapter two: Understanding Nerves

Using nerves to aid your presentations

Understanding Nerves

What are nerves and where do they come from?

Nerves are a side product of the release of a chemical in the brain known as cortisol. Cortisol is an important hormone in the body, secreted by the adrenal glands and involved in the following functions and more:

-Proper glucose metabolism

-Regulation of blood pressure

-Maintenance and immune function

Normally, it is present in the body at higher levels in the morning, and at its lowest at night. Although stress isn't the only reason that cortisol is secreted into the bloodstream, it has been termed "the stress hormone" because it is also secreted in higher levels during the body's 'fight or flight' response to stress, and is responsible for several stress-related changes in the body.

There is a positive and a negative side to nerves. Nerves get adrenaline going. When the adrenaline starts pumping around your body, different things start to happen. We all know the negative ones, such as: light stomach, sweating, shaking, stuttering words, red rash, dry mouth, and a whole lot more.

Understanding why this happens is important to control your nerves. Your brain works a very simple program that it has used for hundreds and thousands of years. Our caveman ancestors were hunters who had to feed their families, the program was running in them and it is still running in us now. When faced with Danger (such as a 10 foot bear with very sharp teeth) the program kicked in and released cortisol. Your body helps by releasing adrenaline; this pumps blood from your extremities to your vital organs, making your heart beat faster, increasing blood flow, and heat generation in the body, causing sweaty hands and the shakes. It also closes down anything that is NOT necessary, like your saliva glands, so your mouth goes dry. It also narrows your focus on what is really important at that point in time (to survive).

So on the positive side, the increase in adrenaline is what gives you the extra energy to deliver a magical presentation, and the sharpness of your senses will help you stay focused.

A number of surveys have been carried out over the years to understand peoples biggest fears, typically the list includes:

- Heights - Spiders- Death- Flying, etc.

All of these are genuine fears that people battle with every day, however, when people are asked to rank their biggest fears in order a strange thing happens. Top of the list is 'Public Speaking' with death coming in at number two.

Now let's just take a look at this statement for a moment. With public speaking at number one, and death at number two, people are saying that they would rather die than deliver a public speech! This does not make sense, especially when asked about public speaking 'what is the worst thing that could happen?' people respond 'I could die'; hold on... that is your number two fear! This is exactly what FEAR is, fear is not rational, it does not make sense (except to the person experiencing it). Fear can be described as:

F - False

E - Evidence

A - Appearing

R - Real

Fear of public speaking is common, however, it is also easy to overcome. There are a number of techniques you can easily use to start to manage your nerves and remove the fear of public speaking.

With public speaking the 'False Evidence' comes from our negative self-talk, we focus on what 'could' go wrong, why we hate presentations, and what mistakes we are going to make. When we focus on these negative aspects we start to worry about what will go wrong and how we are going to fail. This increases the stress levels and causes a potential state of fear.

A much better and more effective way to deal with nerves is to focus on the positives, what will work, how good the presentation will be, the great outcomes from the delivery. Our minds are a wonderful thing, they respond to all of our senses, including our internal thoughts and words. When you focus on the positive your mind also focuses on the positive and 'switches' on the parts of your brain for creativity and success.

There is a wise old saying *'fail to prepare and prepare to fail'*. This is a very true statement. Great presenters know the value and importance of good preparation before a presentation. We will look at preparation in the next chapter, but first we need to look at dealing with nerves through a simple range of effective techniques.

One of the most stressful presentations or speeches people are asked to deliver is that of the 'best man' speech at weddings. People spend weeks worrying and planning. Some even spend money on getting a professional to write it for them. When the big day arrives they worry about the time of the speech, focus on what is going to go wrong, and stress over what people are going to say. Their minds are full of thoughts like, ' *I am not as funny as Joe*', or ' *what if I forget my lines*'. All these negative thoughts have a physical effect on the person. They look stressed, and people notice this. That is when an old tradition kicks in. Someone says '***here, have a bevy***' (a small drink, usually brandy or whiskey) to calm the nerves. The idea behind the 'bevy' is to relax the person and help them through the presentation or speech. This specific tradition has been practiced all over the world for many years.

So instead of fighting against tradition you should embrace it. Yes, have a 'bevy' before a presentation or speech! However, the 'bevy' we recommend is **non-alcoholic.**

The 'bevy' we recommend is:

B - Breathing

E - Emotions

V - Visualise

Y - Yourself

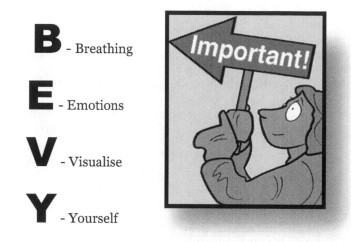

BEVY is a tried and tested formula for success. By applying this simple 4-step process you will learn to manage your nerves and develop good preparation techniques to set yourself up to deliver an excellent presentation. Let's take a closer look at the bevy model:

Breathing:

Doctors, health specialists, and exercise gurus all agree that the easiest way to release stress and nerves is through controlling your breathing. Below you will find a simple breathing exercise that you can practice and perfect to meet your personal needs.

1.   Sit in a comfortable position, you may choose to sit with legs beneath the buttocks with knees directly in front, as some people find this position to be uncomfortable, you may also sit cross-legged or in another position that's more comfortable for you. Even standing in a relaxed position will help.

2.   Close your eyes, but keep your back straight, shoulders relaxed, head up, your eyes (behind your lids) focused ahead.

3.   Take a deep, cleansing breath, expanding your belly and keeping your shoulders relaxed, and hold it in for the count of six. Exhale, and repeat twice more. Then breathe normally, and focus your attention on your breathing. As you breathe, inhale through your nose and exhale through your mouth, still expanding your belly rather than moving your shoulders up and down.

4.   If your thoughts drift toward the stresses of the day ahead or of the day behind you, gently refocus on your breathing and remain in the present moment. Feel the air move in, and feel the air move out. That's it.

If you have a medical condition please consult with your doctor on the correct breathing pattern for you.

Tips for breathing from the experts:

- As you breathe, let your abdomen expand and contract, rather than moving your shoulders up and down. This deeper breathing is more natural and similar to how babies breathe. It gives you increased lung capacity, whereas the 'shallow breathing' adults usually utilize doesn't allow as much oxygenation of the blood.

- Focus on the pace of your breathing, it is not a race, deep slow breaths work best; just breathe at a natural rate, but more deeply.

- If you find your thoughts drifting a lot at first, don't worry that you're doing it 'wrong'. Noticing that you've drifted and refocusing to your breathing is part of the practice, and something you're doing 'right'!

- Block out external distractions, find a quiet space were you can focus and listen to your own breath. Some people find relaxing music helpful. If you want to use music make sure it is soft and low. There are many relaxing tunes available today from a range of providers, find one that works for you.

- Clear your thoughts, empty your mind, simply focus on your breathing, let this take over your complete attention. Feel each breath coming in, flowing through your body, providing clean air to your organs, enjoy the freshness it provides, then slowly release the breath and feel how relaxed you are.

Breathing is the first step in the bevy model. Allowing your system to relax will help you move into the second step.

Emotions:

Our emotions are very powerful; they can drive our actions and behaviours. Professional actors know this and use the power of emotions to turn a performance into an Oscar winning delivery. Take a tip from the professionals and use emotions as part of your bevy routine before presentations.

Think back to a happy time in your life, recall that memory. It may be a great night out, a family trip, a holiday with friends, when you won an award, or when you just felt on top of the world. Take that memory and re-live it. Remember how you looked then, who was with you, the sounds, the scenes, and the way you felt. As you continue to recall this memory make the picture brighter, turn the sound up louder, and take a big breath in and smell the scents from that time.

Now quickly, look at yourself in a mirror if you can. How happy do you look? How good do you feel? Emotions are contagious. They spread throughout our whole bodies quickly. When you run a positive emotion your body responds with positive effects. This is the power of emotions, and you brought on these emotions by simply remembering a happy time in your life. You have the power to trigger emotions through a simple thought. So when preparing for a presentation with the bevy model, identify what emotion you want to feel and remember a time you felt that way. Then bring that memory into your mind and enhance it.

Actors use this technique before a performance. If an actor needs to play a scene where they are angry, they remember a time when they were angry and re-live this moment in time. They allow the emotions they felt at that time to run through their bodies, and when they are ready they step out and deliver an angry performance!

So if you need to feel calm, grounded, confident, or engaging, simply recall a time you felt these emotions. Re-live that experience, amplify the sights, sounds, and feelings you experienced. Bring that picture into your mind and turn it into a live show, turn up the volume, make the picture stronger and experience the emotions again. Let the emotions flow through your body.

Identify the emotions you wish to experience

Once you have the emotions running you can draw on their positive effect to help you deliver your presentation. Focus on the emotions you want to feel and recall the events that will trigger these emotions.

Re-live the experiences that trigger these emotions

Visualise:

The next step in the bevy model is visualisation. Visualisation is a technique drawn from sports psychology. In the world of sports Olympic champions across every discipline have one thing in common. They _believe_ they are the best, they know just how good they are and they picture this over and over and tell themselves just how good they are all the time.

When Sally Gunnell won a gold medal for the hurdles in Barcelona she had ran the race over 400 times in her mind knowing exactly what she would do. When the firing gun sounded, she just hit PLAY on the DVD player in her head, and did what she had done over 400 times already, ran the Olympic final and won the **GOLD** medal.

Visualisation is a very powerful technique. When visualising yourself, do not see it as a movie, seeing yourself from outside, but actually live the moment from inside, be aware of the feelings, the smells, and all of your senses. See the visualisation through your own eyes.

See yourself achieving your goals. Live the experience.

Here is a simple process for visualisation. You can apply the process to whatever goal or outcome you want to experience by following these simple steps:

1. Imagine the outcome you want to achieve, such as a brilliant presentation that receives a standing ovation, or a successful agreement to your proposal. Whatever your goals imagine what it would be like once you achieve them.

2. Take that image and amplify it, see it in full colour, clear sound and live action. See yourself in that situation and imagine what you would feel like.

3. When you have a strong image step into the picture and become yourself, be yourself as you see yourself in the successful situation.

4. When you step into yourself become aware of the sights and sounds around you. Feel the emotions and sensations flowing through you.

5. Stay in the moment and enjoy the experience. Remember what got you here, the success you have delivered and how good it feels.

6. Now start to create all the actions and behaviours that got you to this successful situation. Imagine all the positive things you have done to become successful and achieve your goal.

7. See yourself doing these actions and behaviours; see how they lead you to the success you have achieved.

Once you have a strong visualisation run it over and over in your mind, keep adding richness and clarity to the images you visualise. You can continue to enhance your techniques by adding contingency plans by exploring all possible situations you may face during the presentation.

Yourself:

The final step of the bevy model is being yourself. It is important to feel comfortable during a presentation. The last thing you need to worry about is playing a different role or trying to be someone else. If you are not a stand-up comedian or someone who dances around the stage with the grace of a ballet dancer then why do you need the extra pressure of trying to perform something that you are not comfortable with?

Presentations are about you, be yourself, people know you and are comfortable with you. When you try to be someone else the focus may be lost from the presentation and people may focus on your behaviours more and not pay attention to the message you are delivering. You already have all the tools to deliver a great presentation within yourself, use them.

Being yourself is important, deliver presentations in a style you are comfortable with and is suited for the audience. However, being yourself does not mean **limiting** yourself. Poor presenters use the excuse *'that just is not me'* before even trying a new style or technique. Good presenters try out new styles and behaviours to see what suits them and how they can use different techniques to enhance their presentations. Great presenters build on their natural ability by 'modelling' other presenters they admire. Modelling is just what is says, 'modelling' it is not copying. Trying to be someone else is not the answer. Looking at what they do and how you could use that is much more powerful and effective.

Modelling is a technique where you identify skills, behaviours, and actions you admire in another person (you know, the way they do it), and try it out for yourself.

Modelling is taking what others do and making it your own, crafting it to suit your style and adapting it to your presentations.

To model someone simply identify the actions, behaviours, and methods they use that you admire and look at how they perform. Once you identify what it is they do, and how they do it, you can try it out yourself. Practice these behaviours , find what works for you and suits your style best.

It may even be helpful to identify a mentor who will coach you through your modelling, helping you decide what works best for you.

Find what works best for you through experimentation and practice. Once you find a new technique or tip add it to your toolbox. With a strong bevy in you, you are ready to prepare.

Chapter three: Preparation for Success

A great start leads to an easy journey

3

Preparation for Success

Preparation is the key to great success!

Like it or not, in today's media rich environment, your direct competition in presentations are:

- -Professional presenters (TV, radio)
- -Public speakers
- -Public figures

People are used to seeing professionals deliver the news, information, and advertisements every day.

These presenters all have professional teams surrounding them, perfecting their presentations, writing scripts, applying professional make-up and lighting. If you have ever watched live TV you know just how many things can go wrong, and they usually do. These professionals without their support teams face the same challenges as you.

To help you compete with these three P's (professionals, public speakers, public figures), you can apply your own three P's, and they are:

-Preparation
-Practice
-Perfecting

The first of these, preparation, is vital to the success of your presentations. Before you even start to put a presentation together, there are a number of questions you need to answer. They include:

-*What is the goal of my presentation?*

-*Who will be attending?*

-*What do they need to know?*

-*Why am I presenting?*

-*Where will I be presenting?*

-*Will I be presenting alone, or part of a team?*

-*Will there be other presenters before or after me?*

-*What questions will they ask?*

-*What equipment will I be using?*

-*Do I need to bring any materials?*

-*How long will the presentation last?*

These are just a few of the questions you will need to answer before you start to develop your presentation. At the end of this chapter there is a good preparation checklist for you to use, however, it is strongly recommended that you start to develop your own preparation checklist for your presentations. This checklist should include all the relevant questions for your presentation situations. By completing the checklist you are setting yourself up for continued success.

Goal Setting

The first question to ask yourself is what is the goal of my presentation? What do you want to get out of this? How do you want the audience to feel? What do you need them to do? And what do you want them to think? A great set of questions to ask yourself are:

At the end of this presentation what do I want the audience members:

- **Thinking**

- **Feeling**

- **Doing**

By setting your goals against the desired outcomes of the presentation you will be able to define your goals more clearly.

Spend some time defining your goals. What is your top priority, if you could only achieve one thing from this presentation what would it be? The initial goals you set will shape and direct the rest of your presentation. A good set of goals will allow you to filter out unwanted information later in the development stage. By simply asking *'does this achieve my goals?'* you can identify what information is critical and what is not required.

Think back to your last presentation. What was the goal of this presentation? Did you achieve your goal? What helped or hindered you achieving your goal? What can you learn from this experience to help you set better goals?

Know your Audience:

Think back to the best presentation you attended? Why was this the best, what did the presenter do to make it your best experience?

The best presentations are the ones that have been tailored to meet your needs. The presenter has taken the time to understand you and what you want out of this presentation. The way they design, structure and deliver their presentation has been carefully developed with you in mind. This is a very good strategy.

Always asking *'what is in it for them'* will help you tailor the content and delivery to suit the audience's needs. Knowing who is coming, what are their vested interests, do they have any challenges, and are they opposed to your presentation. Knowing the answer to these questions will help you prepare.

Taking some time to understand who will be attending your presentation will allow you prepare more effectively. Knowing if it will be a hostile or friendly audience will enable you to tailor your presentation to their specific needs and avoid frustrating or upsetting the audience.

What type of audience are you expecting?

As you review the list of audience members ask yourself, what is their opinion on this topic, what questions will they have, what is important to them, will they support or oppose your ideas?

Even if you are presenting to a new or unfamiliar audience you should still run through these questions. Imagine yourself in their shoes and see the world from their point of view. Is there a specific culture or set of behaviours you need to be aware of? What is the dress code? (how you dress will be covered later in this book). Is there any taboo topics you need to avoid? What are they expecting to hear from your presentation, will this conflict with their views?

When you do not know your audience, is there someone else who does know them? Can you find out about the audience?

Location, Location, Location...

Just imagine, you have spent weeks perfecting that Powerpoint presentation, adding fabulous pictures, dazzling graphics, state of the art animations and all the information anyone could need. This little file is your pride and joy. You know you will be successful with this presentation. You arrive nice and early, with your best dress/suit on, hair groomed, your whole act polished to perfection. Your moment arrives, you enter the room, twelve eager and welcoming executives look at you and smile, *yes,* and you have this one nailed...

You head for the top of the room... then you look around for the projector, at first you do not see it, you think, ah... *it must be one of the new ones connected into the wall, or roof.* You ask politely, "where do I set up my laptop?" ... The answer... "Sorry, there is no projection facilities in this room, just go ahead and use the flip chart there..." Your world starts to crumble, the best presentation you ever created will now stay on your laptop, and the audience will never see it. How can you go on without it?

OK, it may not be this extreme, however, hundreds of presenters have arrived at their locations only to find that the room or hall does not have the facilities available to them that they expected. Lighting, sound, podium, etc. to name just a few. Even things as simple as plug socket locations have ruined the potential of some presentations. By knowing your location, you will be prepared for what to expect. In addition to this, professional presenters also have a plan B, plan C, plan D, and so on...

Professional presenters know their venues well, they visit the location before the presentation, practice at the venue whenever possible and memorise the room setup and layout. They know where every squeaky floorboard is, and every blind spot in the room so they can avoid them.

Presenters that leave things to chance usually get a big surprise. You are not a fortune teller; make sure you know the layout of your location.

Make sure you know what your location will be like.

Whenever possible, gain access to the venue before your presentation to get used to the location and setup. If access is restricted or limited ask the venue organiser for a room layout and map. If you are presenting in a hotel make sure you speak to the facilities manager about light, heating, sound, access and emergency exits.

Do you have control over the room layout, what is the best setup for your audience, what equipment is available at the venue and what do you need to bring? What back up materials or equipment are available? If you are using a projector do you know the controls? Where are the spare bulbs if required? Walk around the room; observe the lighting and the temperature. Is there any obstructions or steps you need to be aware of? How do you control the lighting, heating, sound? Where are the restrooms and break facilities. Know your location like your front room.

Timing is everything:

As all performers know, timing is everything. How long is your presentation? Does that include questions? What if the previous person runs over, will you be able to adapt with the time remaining?

Give yourself plenty of time to respond to questions, unexpected interruptions, and any other interventions that may affect the timing of your presentation. A good point to remember is, no one ever gives out for finishing a meeting or presentation early! It is a gift of time back to them. They will thank you for it. If a presentation only takes ten minutes, then schedule it for the right amount of time. Going over time is one of the sins that presenters commit regularly. If the presentation is scheduled to finish at 4pm, from 3:55pm people may be watching the clock. If you run over they may not focus on the message, instead they will remember that you ran over and kept them late for their next appointment.

Make sure you stay on time.   Running late frustrates people.

Remember this simple rule:

Start on time, _stay_ on time, _finish_ on time.

Order of your presentation:

Will you be presenting as part of a team or group? When are you delivering? Are there other presenters before or after your presentation? Will you be presenting before or after lunch? Are you presenting first or last?

The order of your presenting is also important. If you are presenting as part of a group how will you transition from one speaker to the next? Can you arrange the speakers to capture their strengths at the right moment in the presentation? If you are very passionate about the topic when should you present in the order? If you are very factual should you deliver the data section, or if you are creative and engaging would the ideas section suit you best? Ideally group presentations should only have the required number of people presenting. Many presentation groups make the mistake of trying to allow everyone to speak. This may clutter the stage, or draw attention away from the content as people wonder who is up next. The key messages may be lost in the transitions. Great team presentations are delivered by the individuals who can enhance the message at the right point of presentation. You may bring everyone 'on-stage' but not everyone needs to speak. The team can be seated on stage with the designated speakers sitting closest to the presentation area (podium, lectern, or microphone) in the order of presenting.

Great team presentations should be delivered like the performance of a world class relay team. The presentation is the baton, and is passed from team member to team member at fixed points clearly identified for maximum effectiveness without impacting on the overall performance. The order of the presenters, just like the order of the runners in the relay, will be based on their skills and strengths. Who is ideal to open or close your presentation?

You may find yourself presenting before or after other presenters. It is important to know what they will be presenting: will it support or challenge your content? Can you draw on their success or distance yourself from their failings? If the audience agreed with them how can you link to this support? If the audience were bored with their presentation how can you reengage them and help them forget this negative experience?

Presenting with other presenters creates a great opportunity to enhance your own delivery. Even when the topics are different you can draw on the experience they created with the audience. Always acknowledge great presentations, and draw from their content. This can be done by simply saying '*And just as you have seen from Joe, the important aspect is about increasing your profits*' or '*Mary told you about the importance of customer service, now let me show you how you can do this faster, cheaper, and better, than your competitors*'.

The opposite also applies, if someone delivered 'a bomb' that the audience did not like, or if they upset or frustrated the audience, use that to your advantage. Simple statements such as ' *now we have seen how this can be difficult, we know that is not the way to do it, instead let me show you a better way...*' or ' *if you want to experience what the earlier presenter offered you can, however, I know you would much prefer to experience this...*' Here you are using the audiences previous experience to influence them away from what they did not like and offering an alternative that they will love.

When presenting make sure you plan to be present to hear what the other speakers are saying. Even when this is not possible try to do some research around the presenters, can you ask them about their content? Do you know people they have presented to before? The more information you can find out the more preparation you can do to enhance your own presentation.

Remember, preparation is the foundation to a successful presentation.

Planning for questions:

A tough question can derail a presenter who is not prepared to deal with it. An important aspect of preparation is asking yourself:

'What is the worst question they could ask?'

By planning and preparing for tough questions you will develop answers for the *'worst question'* the audience may ask. If it is never asked, then great, however, if it is asked you have already planned for it and will be able to handle it with ease. Great presenters manage the tough questions by building the right information into their presentations. In addition they tackle the tough issues by bringing them out in the presentation and showing the audience they have done their homework and look at both sides of the topic or message they are presenting. Presenters who do not plan for tough questions can be caught off guard or derailed by a tough question. Trying to avoid questions or specific elements of your topic can be just as harmful, standing wide-eyed and open mouthed in response to that one question the presenter had dreaded is not professional.

When you are preparing for a presentation ask yourself what are you not saying? What related areas may come up in questions? Who is attending and what might they ask? What are the key interests of the group? Who supports or challenges my content, and what do they say? By asking these questions you can identify potential questions the audience members may ask. Speak to friends; ask them to ask questions about your topic. A fun way to find questions that might be asked is to present to a small group of people while you are preparing and tell them you have a prize for the toughest questions asked. Reward the tough questions with a sweet or small gift; this will encourage others to ask tough questions. The more they ask, the better prepared you will be for the actual presentation.

Practice makes perfect:

If you want to perfect anything you need to put in the practice work. Even highly successful public speakers practice their delivery over and over until they are happy with every detail of the presentation.

You can practice on your own to develop comfort with the content. Once you are happy with the structure and flow it is time to practice in front of an audience. At first, practice in front of a warm and supporting audience. The goal is to become comfortable delivering to an audience so start off with an audience you know. Ask them to provide positive feedback on what they liked. When you feel ready ask them how you can improve your presentation, what worked, what did not work, and what you could do to make it even better next time.

Professional speakers regularly review video footage of their presentations to observe their delivery. This is highly recommended, however, remember you are your own worst critic so try to identify the positive aspects as well as the areas you wish to improve.

Developing your checklist:

A checklist is a great way to ensure you have covered all the important aspects of your presentation. From who is attending to the equipment you need for delivery a checklist is a helpful tool to capture your key preparation routines.

A checklist should include:

- *The goal of your presentation*
- *What you want the audience thinking, feeling, doing*
- *The 5 W's Why, What, Who, Where, When*
- *The benefits to the audience*
- *Delivery methods and materials/equipment required*
- *Who is coming, what they might ask, why they are here.*

These are just the basics; you should develop your own checklist and expand it as you build experience.

Preparation

What is your goal for this presentation?

By the end of the presentation you want the audience:

Thinking:

Doing:

Feeling:

Fill in the 5 W's below:

WHY	
WHAT	
WHO	
WHERE	
WHEN	

List the Benefits for the audience:

1.

2.

3.

What delivery method will be used?

Electronic	Handouts	Slideshow	Props	Flipchart	OHP
Demonstration	Simulation	Interactive	Lecture	Discussion	Q & A

Who is attending? *(for presentation with larger audience, capture key stakeholders below)*

Name	Position	Comments

A preparation checklist should include all the critical information that will enable you to plan for and develop a strong foundation for your presentation.

Chapter four: Building the Structure

Upon the solid foundation we will build a masterpiece

4

Building the Structure

Structure provides stability, even in a storm!

Structuring presentations consists of putting together the materials you want to deliver in an organised way that flows and adds creditability to you presentation. Your presentation needs structure, it needs:

- *A Start*

- *A Middle*

- *An End*

A simple way of looking at this is when you are structuring your presentation, you want to introduce the audience to your topic, explain your topic, and then showcase the key elements of your topic.

Your structure should flow nicely between the start, through the middle section, and finish up with the ending.

Structure:

The *START* should open with a bang, capture your audience and introduce what it is you are going to talk about. The *MIDDLE* should contain the key points you want to present to your audience. The *END* should summarise the key points and close with a bang, leaving the audience, thinking, feeling, or doing what you set as your goal initially.

START -> MIDDLE -> END

Many presentations lose the audience simply because they are not structured. Audience members like to know where they are going and when. Just like a car trip we want to know where we are going, how we are getting there, and how long it will take. Once we have this basic information we are free to sit back and enjoy the experience. Presentations are the same, once your audience knows what you are going to speak about and how you are going to deliver the presentation they are free to listen and enjoy your delivery.

Structure enables you to add clarity, brevity, and impact to your presentations. Structure helps position information clearly for the audience. Using a structure ensures you stay on topic and do not fall into the trap of 'waffling' or 'losing your message'. Structure provides you with the opportunity to add impact to your key message by building the foundation during the start, exploring options and information in the middle, and delivering the final 'punch' at the end.

Structuring your presentation also helps your time keeping by providing key transition points along the way to keep you on track. If you are tight on time or running over, a structure allows you to 'by-pass' information and jump straight to your key message and the power of your ending.

The Start:

How can you 'hook' your audience? What can you do in the first 30 seconds to captivate the audience? A lot of judgments and decisions are made within the first 30 seconds. You spend the rest of the presentation either confirming or challenging the judgements and decisions in your audience's heads. So starting off on the right foot, having the audience bought in from the start is very important.

Presenters commonly refer to 'starting with a *bang*'. What exactly do they mean by starting with a *bang*? A **'Bang'** is an opening, a unique way to capture the audience. The key to using a **'Bang'** is to start with a *bang* that suits your personality and your subject.

There are 5 main types of bangs which are detailed below.

-The Classic Bang
Introduce your presentation with one or two highlights... *'this new product will save you millions.'*

-The Mystery Bang
Drop in one or two ambiguous clues about your presentation *'this presentation will serve you well if you are ever lost at sea'.*

-The Imagine Bang
Have people imagine a situation, remember a recent event, or picture the future... *'imagine you are on a dark road and your car breaks down..'*

-The Participation Bang
Get the audience involved, ask a question, get them talking to each other, run a quiz, get someone to give input.

-The Dramatic Bang
Use a gimmick/prop, make a provocative comment, use sound, video, pictures, or tell a funny story.

The Middle:

The middle section of your presentation is where you deliver the key points. Depending on the content and topic this may include examples, activities, samples, or audio/visual clips.

The trick is to keep it short! A good rule for presentation content is:

'If in doubt cut it out!'

To help you keep the content crisp, compact, and concise, constantly ask yourself:

> *-What is in it for them?*
> *-What do they NEED to know?*
> *-How can I present this easier?*
> *-Can I show them instead of explaining?*
> *-If I was in the audience what would I like to see/hear?*

I always recall my old English teacher in school offering very wise advice before an exam, he would say *'now, answer the questions briefly, showing your understanding and then stating your reasoning'*. That was it, no waffle, no filling, and no additions just for the sake of it. Good advice, however, we always ignored this advice and wrote pages and pages, trying to get our point across in ten different ways getting as much information as we could on the paper. Give them the facts they need, not the information you would like to give them!

Professional presenters start with a draft structure, and then typically cut 50% of the draft before the final revision. People new to presenting do the opposite, and start with a draft then continue to add to it, and then add again, until it is overloaded with information, text, examples, and waffle.

How much is too much or too little? How can you tell? Remember your P's 'practice'. Get feedback, deliver your presentation to a test audience and ask them.

Selling your ideas:

There is a saying in relation to presentations, *'you are always selling something'*. This is quite true, even if you are not delivering a sales presentation, you are selling either:

-*Your idea*

-*Your Plan*

-*Yourself*

A trick you can adopt from the sales and marketing world is that of the *FAB* model. The *FAB* model stands for Features, Advantages, and Benefits. In sales they focus on the benefits.

James Dyson, inventor of the Dyson vacuum cleaner knows this all too well. After launching his design sales were slow. The advertising campaign first focused on the technical features (cyclone system) then on the advantages of owning a Dyson. The competitors just hit back with their own features and advantages (cheaper). Only when Dyson focused on the benefits did sales take off.

The power of 3:

Have you ever noticed just how many common everyday things are packed into 3's? Some examples are:

-Morning, noon, and night.

-The sun, the moon, the stars.

-The 3 little pigs.

There are hundreds of examples, so why in 3's? Well 3's work well together, it is both rhythmical and memorable, our brain structure likes things in 3's. You can tap into this during your presentations, group things together into 3's, have three key points, and give three examples.

Even for larger presentations look at how you can group items or arguments together into 3's. When influencing show the audience the three main reasons why they should agree with you. Discuss the three main disadvantages of not selecting your idea or option. When asking the audience to make a choice always provide three options.

Influencing:

There are many books on influencing, from using your voice, to appealing to the audience's needs, the trick is to have the audience come around to your way of thinking on their own (otherwise it is manipulation and no one likes to be manipulated). Here are two techniques for increasing influence in your presentations:

1. Options:

As humans we like options, if we do not have options then we are being forced into doing or thinking something. We have a tendency to automatically rebel against this. Always provide your audience with options. You can also provide options that are really not options at all, such as; *'we can do this now or later'*. A good trick is the 3 options reverse. It works like this:

-Always provide 3 options.

One option is not a choice at all, more of a command and people do not like to be told what to do unless in an emergency situation. Two options is forced choice people do not like being forced into anything.

-Position your preferred option third in the list.

Ideally have the least preferred option as number 2 and your back up as option 1.

-Present options 1 and 2 by listing the Pros and then the Cons.

This causes the audience first to be excited by the positives of the option only to be let down by the disadvantages. By placing the con's last this is what they will remember.

-Present option 3 with the Cons first then the Pros.

You can link the cons of option 3 with option 2 by simply saying 'option 3 **also** has cons' you list them and move quickly to the advantages. The audience are left with a positive. Typically people will select the option that leaves them feeling good.

2. The 4-Step Model

Move people away from the current situation or away from a potential situation, show them a great alternative, identify the hazards, and then show them an easy way to get there.

The process is:

1- Create a sense of dissatisfaction with the current events/situation/product etc. People are easily influenced away from danger/loss/hurt/pain etc. Although it does not make sense people are more influenced away from a loss than towards a gain. By starting the process with dissatisfaction you are influencing people away from the current status or away from an alternative option.

2- Paint a bright future by removing the dissatisfaction and showing the benefits of your option(s). Identify what it could be like, how good people would feel if they select your option. Present the benefits first then the option that will deliver these benefits.

3- Reduce any barriers to your options by focusing on benefits. Identify and discuss the barriers but use step 4 to show how you can overcome these barriers by using your option. By showing the barriers you are building creditability with the audience. You are facing up to the reality of the situation and not hiding from the potential barriers.

4- Show the practical and easy steps to achieve this. Present a simple process in stages/steps that introduces, adopts and embeds your option. This simple process should overcome any barriers identified or discussed in step 3.

Use the 4-step model when you need to win over an audience or change their mind-set towards your option.

The direction of influencing:

A quick note on the direction of influencing is important at this point. Think of influencing as either *push* (pushing people towards a specific option) or *pull* (pulling the audience towards an option). Each direction has a set of associated behaviours.

For Push style:
The typical behaviours associated with the push style are telling, selling, or directing. Here you are pushing the benefits or features of your option on the audience, trying to persuade them your option is best.

For Pull style:
The typical behaviours associated with the pull style is asking questions, bridging, agreeing, encouraging, and building connections. Here you are bringing the people with you and explaining your option in relation to their specific needs. Think of it as asking them what they need and tailoring your option to suit these needs.

A word of warning:
People generally do not like to be told what to do. A strong push style can come across as demanding or 'the hard sell' and this may influence people away from your option. Remember people tend to agree with people they like. By building rapport and connection with the audience you are increasing your influence naturally.

The End:

The ending of your presentation is your opportunity to summarise the key points and close with a bang! Leaving your audience with the right lasting impression. They leave the presentation thinking, feeling, or doing what you set as your goal in the first place.

1. *Summarise your key points*
2. *Deal with any open questions*
3. *Finish with a BANG*

Finishing with a bang is very powerful; linking it back into the opening bang is even more powerful. It is important that you do finish with the last word, if you have fielded questions this may deflect from your key messages. People leave the presentation remembering the last question and not your key messages.

Questions, questions, questions

When should you field questions? Some presenters take questions ad-hoc, others only at the end of presentations, while others still choose not to field questions at all.

Here are some tips:

-If you want to field questions, then doing so in a structured way that adds creditability to your presentations. Fielding questions at the end is one such way. However, if someone has a 'burning' question and has to hold it until the end they may not focus on your presentation as they are consumed with their own question.

-Large groups tend to shy away from asking questions (fear of asking the stupid question) provide people with the opportunity to post questions on a board and answer them at the end.

-Allow time for questions, even if not in your structure, as someone will ask one anyway. You can use effective language to control question time, such as ' we have time to take two more questions'...

Here is a standard template that may help you with designing your structure:

Structure

What is the total duration of the Presentation? _____

Overview of Structure:

	START	MIDDLE	END
Hook			
Duration			
Key points			
Comments			

Influencing model used: [   ]

List of expected Questions:

Question	Answer

Memory jogger:

Handouts	Books	Break times
Presentation slides	AV Equipment	Number of Participants
Pre Prepared flipcharts	Pens/Paper	Support materials
Samples	Props	Power Cables/extension lead
Lighting	Sound	Clothes

As with the preparation checklist it is recommended that you develop your own template that helps you structure your presentation.

Chapter five: Delivering with Style

Presentations that capture your audience

5

Delivering with Style

You have the message, deliver it in style!

Delivery of your presentation is all about you. How you present yourself for your presentation is just as important as what is in your presentation. The main points for delivery are:

-*Presenting yourself*

-*Your communication style*

-*Your delivery method/channels*

-*Dealing with questions*

To deliver a 'Presentation' you need to be present! Not just in the room, but present in the moment. You need to be clam, confident, and relaxed, also you need to be smartly dressed (to match the audiences expectations), communicate in a clear, concise manner, and deal professionally with interruptions, questions, and technical setbacks. Easily said, but how to do it is the question.

Presenting yourself:

If you have done your homework during the preparation and structuring stages then you will be well prepared for success. However, if you have failed to prepare, then you are prepared to fail. Having confidence in your materials and content will go a long way towards presenting yourself professionally. To help with nerves remember your breathing techniques, follow the BEVY model and allow yourself plenty of time, do not rush to a presentation, better to be 50 minutes early then 5 minutes late.

Match your dress code to the expectations of the audience, even in settings where casual clothes are the norm a 'smart casual' look will be effective. If in doubt always wear a suit, you can turn a suit into a casual look quickly by taking off a jacket, removing a tie/scarf rolling up sleeves of a shirt/blouse. It is not so easy to turn jeans and a t-shirt into a suit.

Remember, you are running a well-rehearsed presentation, relax, remember to breath and enjoy this opportunity to show the audience how much of a professional presenter you are.

Your communication style:

How you communicate says a lot about you as a presenter. What words you use, how you pace yourself, and how do you communicate in a way the audience will not only like but remember? Here are a few tips to help your communication style.

It is HOW you say it, not just WHAT you say!

Dr Albert Mehrabian conducted extensive studies on communications of feelings and attitudes. In 1981 he published "*Silent Messages*" in which he documented his work on communications.

The study published shows that the influence and impact of what people communicate are down to:

-*The actual words used (only 7%)*

-*The way they are delivered, the tone used (38%)*

-*The body language used to deliver the words (55%).*

Since these findings in the report; behavioural psychologists, communication experts, and linguistics have continued to agree with this work.

Another way of looking at this data is that 7% of your communications is WHAT you say, and a massive 93% is HOW you say it. How many times have you needed to use any of the following statements:

"that's not what I said,..."

"You misunderstood me, ..."

"that's not what I meant, ..."

"what made you think that, ..."

In NLP (*Neuro Linguistic Programming*) there is a common statement, it is: 'The effectiveness of your communication is measured by the outcome that results'. As much as we like to think differently, this is true, you own your communications and you own the effectiveness of it. Make sure your body language and tone of voice support the words you are delivering. Think of the message you are delivering, what do you want the audience thinking, feeling, doing? How can you use the appropriate words, tone, and body language to support these goals?

Chapter 6 will introduce some powerful NLP techniques to help with your voice and body language. In this section we will cover the basics around your voice, eyes, and body language to help you deliver a powerful message during your presentation. Although the words are only 7% once your tone and body language are supporting the message the words become very important. They carry the core message of your presentation and can affect the audiences perception of both you and your message.

Words:

When presenting, some people feel the need to use long, complicated, and aggressive words. Professional presenters use simple language, keep it crisp, and use positive language and tones to deliver their message. Remember to keep your words:

- Short, Simple, and Positive.

Here are three exercises for you to practice using words in your presentations:

Exercise one:

Review the following statements and remove/replace the non-essential words. Your task is to reduce the overall word count without impacting the message.

1- 'the completed output of the report is full and complete'

2- 'the results from last quarter's sales projection forecasts have not fulfilled our expectation'

3- 'we are here today to look into our future and see how our company can be more pro-active and develop synergy while fostering collaboration within our divisions to enhance our customer's experience'.

Now try to reduce the word count in each statement without losing the key messages. Sometimes nerves can cause people to try and use long complicated words to try and show that they are knowledgeable in the topic they are presenting. As you know people do not bring dictionaries to presentations and using these long complicated words will only serve to alienate you from the audience. Use words and terminology they use and understand. Avoid technical jargon (unless they use it themselves). Keep it simple.

Exercise two:

Review the list of words below and replace with clearer words (simple words).

Original words   Alternative word (your choice)

Demonstrate   ->
Terminate   ->
Pertaining to   ->
Procrastinate   ->
Circumvent   ->

You may have chosen words such as; show, end, regarding, delay, or avoid. Whichever words you did use to replace the original just make sure they are simple and easily understood.

Exercise three:

Finally, review the statements below and replace with positive statements. Your goal is to develop a positive tone while still delivering the message.

'That presentation was terrible, the slides are good, you should have just sent it out as an attachment, you looked like a nervous wreck up there'

'We did not hit our figures again this week, so what is your excuse this time?'

Keeping your message positive is important. You want the audience to be in a positive frame of mind when listening to your presentation. Being positive does not mean ignoring the facts. If you are dealing with a difficult situation do not brush over the negative facts, instead deliver them as they are. Being positive when you are delivering a negative message may come across as disrespectful to the audience. Instead match your tone and words to the audiences need.

Voice, Eyes, Body Language:

Three areas where presenters can make the most effective impact on their performance are:

-Voice
-Eye contact
-Body language

By making simple changes in these areas the resulting improvements can enhance a presentation and help you achieve your goal. First we will look at how to use your voice more effectively.

Voice:

You can take '***STEPS***' to improve your voice during presentations. STEPS stands for:

Here are the STEPS for improving your voice:

Speed:
Vary the pace of your voice, slow down for clarity and impact, speed up for adding drama. Speed adds movement to your words, bring the audience on a joyful journey. Remember to add rhythm and timing to your speed.

Tone:
Vary the tone of your voice, practice by speaking like a big giant, or a little fairy... read stories and try to take on the voices of the characters. Match the tone of your voice to the emotion of the message you are projecting.

Emotions:
Use emotions in your voice, appealing to people, being happy, sad, energised, or focused; by using these emotions through your voice it will add creditability to your presentation.

Projection:
The audience came to hear you, make sure they do, project your voice out to the room. Even a whisper can be heard when it is projected. You do not need to shout. Projecting your voice comes from your diaphragm, imagine you are pushing your words out against a strong breeze.

Silence:
To add impact, allow information to settle in, or to let people reflect, silence is a powerful technique during presentations. If you ask a question, make sure you give the audience time to answer.

STEPS is a great way to develop your voice and become comfortable with changing speed, tone, and adding emotions. A great way to practice your steps is through reading any children's story book.

Practicing your steps:

Read the following extract from the popular story 'Little Red Riding Hood'. Make sure you emphasize the voices and the situation through applying the STEPS model.

Once upon a time, there was a little girl who lived in a village near the forest. Whenever, she went out, the little girl wore a red riding cloak, so everyone in the village called her Little Red Riding Hood. One morning, Little Red Riding Hood asked her mother if she could go to visit her grandmother as it had been awhile since they'd seen each other. *"That's a good idea,"* her mother said. So they packed a nice basket for Little Red Riding Hood to take to her grandmother. *"Remember, go straight to Grandma's house,"* her mother cautioned. *"Don't dawdle along the way and please don't talk to strangers! The woods are dangerous."* *"Don't worry, mommy,"* said Little Red Riding Hood, *"I'll be careful."*

But when Little Red Riding Hood noticed some lovely flowers in the woods, she forgot her promise to her mother. She picked a few, watched the butterflies flit about for a while, listened to the frogs croaking and then picked a few more. Little Red Riding Hood was enjoying the warm summer day so much, that she didn't notice a dark shadow approaching out of the forest behind her...

Suddenly, the wolf appeared beside her. *"What are you doing out here, little girl?"* the wolf asked in a voice as friendly as he could muster. *"I'm on my way to see my Grandma who lives through the forest, near the brook,"* Little Red Riding Hood replied.

Remember to use STEPS while reading these stories. Change your voice to portray different characters, add speed and emotion to convey the situation. Read these stories to children, they will love it and you will have a willing audience that will give you instant feedback.

Eyes:

Making connection with people through eye contact is very powerful; you can use this to your advantage during presentations. Below you will find three simple techniques for eye contact during presentations. When making eye contact remember this simple model:

The SCR model (Sweep, Connect, Read) will help you with eye contact making it look and feel natural. Here are a few tips for using the SCR model.

Sweep the room

Make sure you are sweeping the room making eye contact with everybody. It is easy just to focus in on a friendly face or to avoid someone you find challenging. Make sure you keep everyone within your eye contact, if you step into the audience remember people to the sides are outside your range, make sure to re-connect and establish eye contact with them.

Avoid the 'lighthouse' or 'goldfish' effect. This is where you simply scan the room from right to left (or left to right) repeatedly in the same motion over and over. People will notice this and see you are not really trying to make eye contact just running through a process.

Connect with people

To avoid the 'goldfish' when sweeping the room (sweeping the room right to left, and repeat...) stop randomly and connect with individuals, a facial gesture can add impact. Make sure you are connecting with different people and avoid just connecting with the same person all of the time.

Read your audience

While sweeping the room and connecting with people, take a moment to read their body language, it speaks volumes. Are people disconnected, chatting, or focused on your presentation? Adjust your style and delivery based on the feedback you are getting.

The nose trick

If you are uncomfortable with direct eye contact, while you are developing these skills try the trusted nose trick. Simply sweep the room and look at the tip of people's noses. Try it, it looks like you are making eye contact, it works and nobody nose... (Sorry for the pun...)

Body Language:

You could fill a small library with the books that have been written on body language. For presentation skills we will focus on the fact that during a presentation you are always on SHOW.

The SHOW model stands for:

- *Style*
- *Habits*
- *Orientation*
- *Walk*

Style:

How do you look? Do you ever catch yourself in the mirror and compliment yourself on how well you look? Make sure you are standing tall, presenting yourself with confidence, practice in front of a mirror, smile more, and open your body. What do you do with your hands? Do you have a rest position?

Habits:
We all have them, from scratching that spot, to clicking the pen. Habits can take away from your presentation. You can make yourself aware of the common ones and avoid these, however nothing beats feedback, especially visual feedback, such as watching yourself on video.

Orientation:
You are presenting to your audience, not the screen, not your notes, not the podium. Make sure you are facing the audience, when you do need to turn away do not continue to present, pause and reposition yourself then continue to present. From time to time you may want to step away (during a video, or visual so the screen is the main focus for the audience), this is fine. When you are ready step back into position and continue.

Walk:
You own your space, use it. Avoid hiding behind podiums, flip charts or desks. Step out and use the space you have to enhance your presentation. Make sure your movement is natural and never pace. Movements that are not natural distract the audience.

A note on hands.
Your hands can help deliver a powerful presentation, use them effectively. Use your hands to emphasize your message and to add movement and visual effects. Picture a box running from your shoulders to your hips, once your hands stay within this area they will not distract the audience. Find a comfortable rest position when you are not using your hands to convey your message. Pick one that is natural for you.

Above all, visual feedback is the most powerful way to raise your awareness about your own body language. Try video recording your presentations, watch it back and see what you observe. Remember that we are our own worst critics so go easy on yourself. Try to look for the positive first, then look at what you need to improve.

Delivery method/channel:

How do you plan to deliver the presentation? Will you use visual aids, video, audio, or hand-outs? Will you be presenting the facts or telling a story? Maybe you want to make the presentation interactive with the audience contributing, or will you use props and samples. Will you provide a demonstration or allow people to try it for themselves?

These questions should be dealt with during the preparation stage. It is important to design your presentation around your goals and select the best way to present your presentation to achieve these goals. If you are using technology to deliver your presentation do you have a back-up plan if the technology does not work?

To help you decide which method or channel is best for your presentation, here are a few key points to remember.

- *Some people want to see the message*

- *Some people want to hear the message*

- *Some people want to experience the message.*

We all have different channels we prefer to receive information on. If you have a friend visiting from a different country what information would you give them for directions to your house? Would you:

- *Tell them how to get to your house (Auditory)*

- *Draw a map (Visual)*

- *Pick them up at the airport (Kinaesthetic)*

You probably picked the one you prefer, but would your friend prefer this method over another? A common mistake presenters make is to present through the channel they prefer the most. Professional presenters deliver through a mixture of channels to ensure they are meeting everyone's needs.

Visual - Auditory - Kinaesthetic:

These are the three primary communication channels. When you are delivering your presentation make sure you communicate on all channels. Delivering with a mixture of visual, auditory, and kinaesthetic will help keep your audience engaged and provide a clear message.

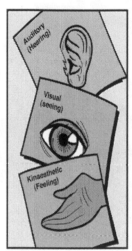

Visual: People who want to see your message will enjoy pictures, video, colour, and graphics. Use posters and colourful flip charts to add visual effects. Download video clips to play and use graphics/pictures to show data.

Auditory: People who want to hear your message will enjoy facts, figures, sounds (including music and audio recordings), and text. Explain the information, use music to enhance the message, play a recording promoting your topic. Provide people with additional hand-outs.

Kinaesthetic: People who want to experience your presentations will enjoy stories, demonstrations, activities, samples, interaction, and role playing. Reach out and touch the audience through engagement, stories, and activities. Get them involved, trying out your ideas or products. Let them experience the presentation.

Using presentation software.

There are many software packages available to help you deliver presentations. They all support visual, auditory, and kinaesthetic channels. Find one that is right for you and learn how to use it. A word of caution - do not over do the animation as this can distract from your presentation. Also keep the slide count and content short. No one enjoys reading hundreds of slides packed with text.

Dealing with Questions:

The last section of this chapter will address how to deal with questions. Poor presenters fear questions and try to avoid them. Great presenters plan for and welcome questions. Remember during your preparation you have already identified the worst questions they could ask!

Dealing with questions using a structured approach adds creditability to your presentations. Below you will find four main strategies for dealing with questions. Professional presenters use all four styles, selecting the one that best suits the situation.

Use a mix of the following strategies to handle questions. Avoid over relying on any one style.

Reflect:
Reflect the question back to the person who asked it. Do this in a positive way, use language such as, 'interesting question, I would love to hear your ideas or thoughts around this'.

Deflect:
Deflect the question to the larger group, sometimes known as the overhead question, you open it up to the room, looking for the input of others. Your language is also important here, try 'excellent, let's see what options other people may consider here...'

Answer:
Yes, it sounds obvious, however some presenters forget to answer the question asked. If you have the answer and it does not detract from your message, then answer it. If however the answer may take from your creditability you may choose to bridge to a more positive answer. Be careful of bridging, if overused people can become frustrated as you are not answering their questions (used by some public figures...)

Follow up:
If you do not have the answer and deflect/reflect are not suitable for this situation, then ask for clarification on specifics and commit to follow up with details. It is fine not to know some answers. The important thing to remember is to follow up and answer the question. Some presenters choose to respond by e-mail and copy other audience members.

You are now on your way towards delivering powerful presentations without fear. The next chapter will explore some advanced techniques you may want to apply to your presentations.

Chapter six: Presenting with Impact

Take a bow and do as the professionals do.

6

Presenting with Impact

Add power and polish to your presentation!

In the previous chapter we covered the basics around presentation delivery for:

- *Voice*
- *Eyes*
- *Body Language*

This chapter will explore some advanced techniques around using your voice and body language that will help you add a professional finish to your already well structured and prepared presentation. Remember the BEVY model and being yourself but not limiting yourself. Apply that approach to the tips and tricks in this chapter. Try them out, see what works for you and identify how you can use these techniques in your presentations.

Voice movement:

Your voice is a powerful tool during a presentation. We have already seen how using the STEPS model can enhance your voice delivery, now we will look at adding movement through your words.

By applying inflections to your words you can change their meaning or enhance their impact. Inflections are simply how you emphasize the last word of your sentence. You can change your tone to:

- ***go up with the last word*** (*implies a question*)

- ***stay flat with the last word*** (*implies a statement*)

- ***go down with the last word*** (*implies a command*)

When you go up with the last word this implies a question, staying flat changes it to a statement and going down will change the sentence to a command.

Let's try it:

Try saying the following using up/flat/down on the last word.

"This is what you do" put the emphases on <u>DO</u>.

You will notice how the meanings of the words change by simply changing the inflection of the last word. This is a very powerful technique when used correctly (one of the verbal/auditory skills in hypnosis). Try it out for yourself and see how it fits you. Identify where you can use these inflections to add influence to your words as you are presenting.

You can also include body language to enhance the delivery, such as raised eyebrows for questions, open hands for statements, closed fists for commands.

Presuppositions:

Another way to enhance communications is through the use of presuppositions. Presuppositions are a way of including information as a given, to bypass a question or choice.

Children are naturally gifted at the use of presuppositions, for example how would you respond to the following question when you arrive home from work to a young son or daughter:

'Hi, welcome home, do you want to play now or later?'

See the presupposition here? Yes they have you, either way you are going to play. The presupposition here is you ARE going to play, the choice is simply now or later. How can you use this powerful technique in your presentations?

Human Filters:

We all have filters running in our brain, it is important you know and understand these filters. Knowing and understanding these filters will allow you to bypass them and make sure your information not only goes in but also sticks. There are over 2 million bits of information being received through your 5 senses all the time, what you see, hear, feel, smell and taste. 2 million bits of information is a massive amount to be arriving in the nervous system every second of the day. In order to keep you from perpetual overload, you have developed three processes to cope with all this information, they are:

Deletion – Generalisation – Distortion

Deletion:

You limit your awareness and deal only with what is important to you at that point in time. You select parts of the information that is coming in and filter out the rest. The information is deleted from your conscious awareness.

Have you ever been so deeply engaged in a book or paper that you are oblivious to somebody asking you a question? What about the clothes you are wearing? Are you aware of the feel of them against your skin? How about the taste in your mouth?

Generalisation:

You also reduce the amount of information you are dealing with by generalising it. Humans are very good at noticing patterns, regularities, and creating abstract principles and rules. Classic examples are objects such as chairs and pens, even though their physical appearance can vary enormously. Another common use of generalisation is "Tarring with the same brush" such as "all politicians are liars".

Distortion:

We also distort information; put our own spin on it. We make connections between what we perceive, and what it might mean. We remember things as we have seen/heard them.

How can you bypass these filters? Bring your information into people's senses by appealing to all the communication channels (Visual, Auditory, and Kinaesthetic). Make your information stand out from the crowd; ensure there is no way it can be dismissed with a generalisation. Find out how the audience perceives your information, blend with their views and redirect back to your key message. A great trick is to *agree with and return to*. To use this simply listen to what a person says and then agree with their statement and redirect back to your point. for example: ' Yes, and it can also be used to...'

The NLP voice pattern:

In the last chapter we introduced the three communication channels of Visual, Auditory, and kinaesthetic.

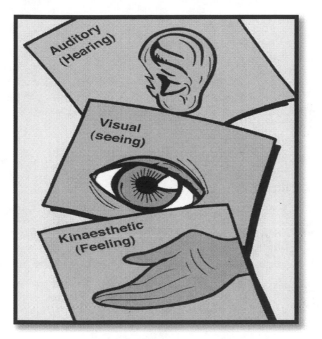

Remember:

-Visual people like to SEE information.

-Auditory people like to HEAR information.

-Kinaesthetic people like to EXPERIENCE information.

In the early days of NLP, researchers studied various speakers that had impact and influence, such as, John F Kennedy and Martin Luther King. From these studies a strategy known as the *charisma pattern* was drawn.

The charisma pattern:

Charismatic speakers start with kinaesthetic, move into auditory, and then visual. This is known as the KAV model.

- *Kinaesthetic first*
- *Auditory second*
- *Visual third*

They do this by starting in a slow low pitched voice with pauses to engage with kinaesthetic people, then speeding up and appealing to auditory people, and finally moving into visual.

To support the KAV model charismatic speakers use specific words that appeal to each one of the channels. They do this because they know that:

Kinaesthetic people want to *experience* your information, they will like the *feel* of it, they do not want it to leave a bad *taste* in their mouth. They will have a *gut feeling* about what is right. (Notice the use of kinaesthetic words in italics).

Auditory people will want to *hear* your information. They will like the *sound* of it, the information may *ring* a *bell* for them. (Notice the auditory words in italics).

Visual people will want to *see* your information. They will like the *look* of it. They need you to *paint* a *picture* for them. They want to *look* at your points and compare *views*. (Notice the use of visual words in italics).

The charismatic speaker uses kinaesthetic words during the kinaesthetic phase, then auditory words during the auditory phase, and visual words during the visual stage.

More information on the preferred channels:

To help you discover and explore the different preferred channels or communication systems, here is some additional information including a range of useful words from each channel.

Visual preferred system:

When communicating to these people use visual language, show them pictures, videos, brochures illustrated with photographs or diagrams, and tell them how things look from your point of view. 'Paint Pictures' with your words:
"How do you see this? Can you picture this? What do you envision? Keep an eye on this, get the whole picture, and then just give me the highlights."

Example of Visual words

See	Look	Hazy	Observe	Flash	View
Picture	Misty	Image	Show	Vision	Focus
Scan	Gaze	Scene	Opaque	Watch	Highlight
Glitter	Vivid	Bright	Insight	Dawn	Glowing
Mirror	Show	Reveal	Glimpse	Sparkle	Envision

Auditory preferred system:

These people notice how things sound. They like listening to people talking to them, telling them stories, either live, or on audiotapes. They are attuned to voice tonality, which may be music to their ears, or sound hollow, or even tongue-in-cheek. They listen out for others speaking their language. Make sure your communication sounds good to them: play them music, or jingles, use a rich voice tonality, and talk to them using words to do with sounds: 'how does this sound to you? Does it strike a chord with you? Are you tuned into these themes?' Sound these people out. Find out if they are on the same wavelength.

Example of Auditory words

Hear	*Say*	*Speak*	*Shrill*	*Loud*	*Listen*
Click	*Talk*	*Chat*	*Sound*	*Noise*	*Tone*
Sniff	*Quite*	*Cadence*	*Accent*	*Melody*	*Musical*
Tune	*Buzz*	*Tell*	*Call*	*Clash*	*Ring*
Shout	*Echo*	*Chime*	*Babble*	*Jingle*	*Screech*

Kinaesthetic preferred system:

These people have more of a feeling for things; use a hands-on approach, so they can grasp the essentials while sifting through a mass of information. They are fascinated and challenged with how things fit together, by organising the stuff someone has dumped on them. No need to handle them with kid gloves: make contact by physically touching them, and use language that touches on feeling: do you have a feel for this? Does it grab you? Put your feelers out. Dig down. Get hold of the essence. And give me your impression, so that I can get a handle on it.

Example of Kinaesthetic words

Feel	*Touch*	*Smooth*	*Solid*	*Rough*	*Grab*
Gritty	*Tight*	*Uptight*	*Pull*	*Handle*	*Pushy*
Soft	*Move*	*Grasp*	*Tough*	*Thrust*	*Rub*
Heavy	*Sharp*	*Tickle*	*Sticky*	*Firm*	*Itchy*
Bounce	*Mime*	*Concrete*	*Hit*	*Dig*	*Slimy*

There is one additional preferred system in the NPL model. This system/channel is known as Auditory - digital. Auditory-digital people have no preference across the first three NLP channels of Visual, Auditory, or Kinaesthetic.

Auditory-digital preferred system:

These individuals will be talking to themselves about the logic, sense, and rationality, of the information being provided. They want factual data with validating numbers and statistics. They consider the theoretical implications through logical analysis, and structured arguments. They make inferences, and project trends based on extrapolating the data under consideration. When communicating with the typical auditory-digital person, use non-sensory words, words that are 'neutral' with regard to any particular sensory system: 'will you find out, and let me know what you think about this? Go and explore this area, and consider the implications of what you're discovering, and provide me with a report that will increase my understanding.'

Example of Auditory-digital words

Basic	*Specific*	*Idea*	*Learning*	*Procedure*
Usual	*Modular*	*Obvious*	*Model*	*Incremental*
Know	*Balanced*	*Virtual*	*Think*	*Knowledge*
Logic	*Random*	*Expert*	*Variable*	*Special*
Theory	*Typical*	*Optimal*	*Boundary*	*Excellent*

Developing all your channels/systems:

A great way to practice developing all four channels is to tell stories. Start with using just one channel, say Visual only, then after a minute switch to another channel, say Auditory only. Continue switching between channels (telling the same story) until you are comfortable with using the different words. Then try to tell stories with the KAV model. You can practice this with friends in a small group. You will be amazed at the creativity of the stories that people can make up through this process.

Using Anchors:

The use of anchors (a way to lock in information) is common in NLP. There are three main types of anchors, they are:

- *Spatial Anchors*
- *Auditory Anchors*
- *Kinaesthetic Anchors*

Spatial Anchors:

Spatial anchors can be used to associate and lock in information, an emotion, or an unspoken word with a physical location within the room. For example you can walk towards the exit and gesture towards the door as you tell people about leaving the room. If you do this 2-3 times people will start to associate leaving the room anytime you walk or gesture towards the door. Think about what you want to anchor in and then pick a spot in the room and anchor that item to the identified spot. You may want to change voice tone to emphasis the item.

A very effective trick used by sales people is to discuss general good things when standing in a specific spot using specific body language and tone of voice. Then they move to the opposite side to discuss all the negative things (again changing body language and tone). When they want to present two offers they will present one from the 'Bad' spot with the associated body language and tone, then move to presenting the alternative option from the 'Good' spot with the associated body language and tone. Guess which one most people will pick? Yes, that is right the option they have associated all the GOOD things with!

Experienced NLP practitioners can produce the same response with just their hands. Presenting one option on one hand with body language and tone, and the opposite on the other hand. (After building the anchors first.)

Auditory and Kinaesthetic Anchors:

The process is similar for both auditory and kinaesthetic anchors. With auditory anchors you associate the items with a sound (the tone of your voice, a sound, or music). Some people present one option in a deep slow voice and other options in a higher squeaky voice (that may irritate audience members), again guess which one most people may pick?

With Kinaesthetic anchors you associate the item with physical contact; it might be a shake of the hand, or placing your hand on a shoulder. A word of warning, unless the audience are comfortable with physical touch you may want to reserve this one for your one-to-one situations where you will not be invading their personal space.

Building rapport:

Rapport is the process that allows you to communicate and bond with your audience's unconscious mind. It removes barriers and opens people to really listening to you. Establishing rapport is the foundation that great presentations are built on.

Rapport occurs when you match other peoples behaviours, thinking, or levels of energy.

Tad James PhD, a master trainer for NLP believes that when people are like each other , they like each other.
How to create rapport:

-Use words they use

-Have empathy with them

-Match their energy

-Adopt the same physiology

-Find shared experiences

Managing your state:

Your state affects your performance, your performance effects your state. So how can you manage this? Your physiology also affects your state and vice versa, and it is easy to change and manage your physiology. Stand up, walk around, smile, and laugh.

Now, think about a time in your life you have been angry with someone, recall why you are angry. OK, how do you feel? What are you doing? What expression is on your face?

Now, stand up, look up at the roof, tense all the muscles in your body, smile wider then you ever have before, really wide teeth and all... now say through your smile, YES, YES, YES...Now how do you feel ?

You can also affect other people's state, first it is important to match (or close to) their state then start to change your own and they will come along with you. Have them change their physiology, remember a past event, dream about the future etc.

Powerful body-language

Virginia Satir, a family therapist, developed an effective way of working with whole families together. From her studies 5 categories have been documented. They are:

The Leveller: Symmetrical physiology: upright, moving hands, palms down, in a downward movement and spreading. e.g. "this is the way it is", "this is true".

The Placater: Symmetrical open physiology, palms up, moving in and upward direction.
e.g. "help me", "I'm open", "I want to please you".

The Blamer: Asymmetrical: leaning forward, and pointing the finger. e.g. "It's your fault", "It's down to you".

The Computer: Asymmetrical, hand on chin or arms folded, thinker pose, academic lecturer stance. e.g. "I'm the authority", "I'm reasonable, logic and sensible"

The Distracter: Asymmetrical physiology, angular, disjointed and incongruent. e.g. "I don't know", "it's not my fault".

Try out these techniques, see what works for you. Remember the BEVY model and be yourself, but do not limit yourself. I hope you enjoy delivering memorable presentations.

Psychological Judo:

In chapter one we made reference to *'Psychological Judo'* as a technique for dealing with difficult participants. Psychological Judo is a technique where you use the strength of the other person against them mentally.

Judo means 'the gentle way' it was developed in Japan as an alternative to the lethal Samari combat arts. Judo uses your opponent's strengths against them to unbalance and defeat the opponent. Psychological Judo uses the same principles to unbalance and defeat your difficult participant or audience member. You simply use their own strengths against them. Here are a few examples of how to apply Psychological Judo.

Dealing with the 'know it all'

The 'know it all' is an expert in their field, use this expertise and encourage their input. Never be afraid of the 'know it all' or worry they will disagree with you. Right from the start of the presentation acknowledge their expertise and ask them to contribute to your materials. By allowing and encouraging their input you are building rapport with the 'know it all' and they will respond with supportive behaviours. You may want to open your presentation with a statement such as *'Thank you for coming along today, we are very lucky to have John here with us today as he is an expert in this area and I am sure he would be delighted to answer any questions I may not have his level of experience in.'*

A great trick to remember is that no one ever argues with their own information. Use this to your advantage, make statements such as: *' As John said at last week's meeting...'*

Dealing with the 'NO person'

We have all attended meetings or presentation where one of the audience members is completely against the idea being presented and sits there with a negative face and body language just waiting for the opportunity to hijack the presentation with their objections.

Again use this against them: encourage their negativity allow them to object. Start off by saying: ' *I fully understand that Joe has some very important concerns around this topic, Joe I would love for you to push me as hard as you can because I want to make sure I have covered all the possible areas'*.

By allowing their negative input you automatically disarm their attack. If they choose to constantly complain the rest of the audience will see this as whining and support your ideas and position more and they will see the constant negativity in the NO person's argument.

When the 'NO person' shifts to just whining it is time to employ another Psychological Judo technique.

Dealing with the 'Whiner'

A whiner is a person that sees a cloud on every silver lining. No matter what you present they will whine about it. A whiner is not looking to generate solutions; they simply want to complain about the current situation.

Use this against them by asking them what they would do, how they see the problem or how they would tackle issues. The whiner will get uncomfortable with this as they do not want to look at solutions. Keep them focused on outcomes and solutions, they will soon stop whining.

Dealing with the 'Talker'

One of the most distracting things that will happen to you while presenting is when one of the audience members constantly talks to the person beside them in a low voice or whisper. The talker can draw your attention away from your presentation and cause you to lose focus.

The psychological Judo technique to apply here is to allow the talker to chat. Encourage comments and questions between audience members. Remember the talker may be asking a question or clarifying a point. A good way to allow this chat is to invite the audience to 'Pair & Share'. When you notice a talker stop what you are doing and ask the audience to take a moment to discuss the current topic/question/statement with the person beside them. Continue to do this every time you see the talker about to chat. They will soon notice a pattern and reduce the amount of chatting they do.

Another way to address this during a presentation is to use the space available in the room. The SHOW model in chapter five discusses the importance of 'walking around' the room and using your space. When you notice 'a talker' simply move over towards them while presenting, you can even step behind them and raise your voice slightly. Continue to do this every time they chat and they will soon stop as they notice you move towards them every time they chat or talk.

If all else fails use the classic interrupt by saying their name. It is very difficult for people to ignore their own name; this is a powerful interrupt technique. It is important you use this technique safely, you do not want to put them under pressure or cause discomfort by 'catching them out not listening' like your old school teachers used to do.

To use this technique safely look at another person in the room and say ' just like Joe said to me last week....' then turn towards Joe and make eye contact. This allows the talker (Joe) to refocus when they hear their name before you draw attention to them.

Dealing with the 'Fidget'

Have you ever sat through a presentation where the person next to you constantly fidgets, it is very distracting to you so imagine how distracting it is for the presenter! Fidget's love to do things, they hate sitting still even for a minute.

Use this to your advantage. Hand out props and samples. Engage the audience with materials they can use to enhance the message you are delivering. Use engaging activities like handing out a set of statements and asking the audience to arrange them in order of importance or grouping them into the statements they agree or disagree with. Have audience members get up and capture notes on a flip chart or generate ideas in small groups. Look for engaging ways to include the audience in your presentation. These simple techniques will flood the fidget with things to do and they will not be distracting the presenter or the other audience members.

These are just a few examples of how to apply Psychological Judo during your presentations to deal with difficult audience members. Remember the trick is to use their strengths against them. Look at what they are doing and see how you can encourage this behaviour or engage the behaviour in a way that supports your presentation.

Chapter seven: Additional Information

Where to go next, what to do...

7

Additional Information

You have mastered presenting without fear, what is next for you?

Congratulations you have reached the final section. This short chapter provides information on where to go next and what to do to continue your presentation skills development. In this chapter you will find:

- Using Powerpoint
- Useful web links
- Recommended reading
- Practice techniques

There are hundreds of excellent web sites and books relating to presentation skills. This section will list just a few of the highly recommended ones. You are encouraged to explore for yourself the range of readings and useful web sites. Enjoy continuing your development.

Using Powerpoint

There are many different software tools available on the market today to aid you in delivering a presentation. One of the most popular tools available is Microsoft's PowerPoint. As discussed in chapter one YOU are the presentation, the software tools you use are a presentation aid, do not use them as a crutch. Here are a few of the basic tips to help you get the most out of presenting using Powerpoint software:

Blanking the screen:

If you do not use a presentation pointer (also known as a slide clicker, used to remotely control the transition of the slides without using the keyboard), then it is important to know how to blank out the presentation when required. When in slide presenter mode in Powerpoint simply press the 'B' key to black out the screen, or the 'W' key to white out the screen. If you are in a room with low lighting conditions it is recommended to white out the screen as blacking out the screen my leave the room in darkness without the light from the projector.

It is a powerful technique to blank out the screen when you want to draw the audience's attention away from the slide projection.

Know your numbers:

When developing a slide presentation keep note of the slide numbers and the content. When in presenter mode Powerpoint allows you to jump directly to a specific slide by entering the slide number on the keyboard and pressing enter. For example if you want to go to slide 8, then simply type the number 8 on the keyboard and press enter, the slideshow will jump directly to slide 8. This gives a very professional look to your presentations and avoids clicking through several slides to get to a specific slide (you may need to jump backwards to re-visit a previous slide).

The last slide:

Always copy and paste the last slide at least 3 times into your presentation. This is a great technique to avoid your slideshow shutting down after the last slide if you press a key by accident. If you do press a key (on the keyboard or pointer) the same slide stays in view on the projector screen and the audience are unaware of the slide transition. If you are nervous and using a pointer it may be wise to copy and paste the last slide up to 10 times, that way even if you continuously click the pointer through nerves the audience will not notice this as the projected slide will not change. Alternatively simply put the pointer down once you are finished.

Running out of time:

If your presentation needs to finish and you have not reached your final slide (with the reminder of your key message), simply press the END key on the keyboard and this will jump straight to the last slide.

Embedding audio/video

Powerpoint allows you to insert both audio and visual files, a great way to add effects to your presentation. Try out different techniques before you use audio or video in a presentation to make sure you have mastered the technique. Earlier versions of Powerpoint (pre office 2010) may only allow linking to the audio or video file so make sure you have the original files with you.

A quick note on presentation pointers:

If you want to use a wireless pointer to automatically transition the slides it is strongly recommended to purchase a robust and simple pointer. There are many models available on the market today, however, keep it simple, go for a pointer with the basic functions of forward, back, and blank out. More complex functionality (including automatic timers) is available but be aware the more functions the device has the more things that may go wrong.

web links:

Here is a selection of useful presentations skills web sites. Please explore the internet to find additional sites that may be beneficial to your needs. These sites are 100% certified.

Site:
http://www.presentationmagazine.com/

Description:
A great resource for FREE tips, tricks, and templates. Full of useful information and practical help for a range of presentation situations and public speaking events.

Site:
http://www.businessballs.com/presentation.htm

Description:
A very helpful site full of examples and training tools. Businessballs is also a great general management and business resource.

Site:
http://www.leadersinstitute.com/

Description:
A commercial site that sells training, however, they do offer a range of free tips and tricks that can be downloaded for free.

Site:
http://www.presentation-skills.biz/

Description:
Similar to presentation magazine, full of tips, tricks, and templates on presentation skills and public speaking.

Site:
http://www.effective-public-speaking.com/

Description:
Free training via e-mail from a training professional.

Site:
http://www.thinkonyourfeet.com/

Description:
Another commercial site, they have a great technique for developing your structure and dealing with difficult questions.

Site:
http://www.public-speaking.org/

Description:
A good site for public speaking tips and tricks, full of free tools and templates.

Site:
http://www.mindtools.com/CommSkll/PublicSpeaking.htm

Description:
Mindtools is another great business resource. They have a good section on public speaking and presentation skills.

Site:
http://www.toastmasters.org/

Description:

The international site for toastmasters. Find a local chapter and meet like-minded people, develop your skills and share your stories.

Suggested books:

-The Definitive Book of Body Language
Allan & Barbara Pease

-Effective Communication
Steve Shipside

-The Handbook of Communication Skills
Owen Hargie

-Present Yourself with Impact
Caryl Winter

-Words that Work
Frank I Luntz

-Voice Power
Grant Williams

-Perfect your Presentations
Steve Shipside

-Brilliant Presentation
Richard Hall

-Openers and Closers Pocketbook
Alan Evans and Paul Tizzard

-The Secrets of Successful Speaking & Business Presentations
Gordon Bell

-Successful Presentations in a Week
Malcolm Peel

-Presenting Magically
Dr Tad James

-What Every Body is Saying
Joe Navarro

Practice techniques:

Every communication you have is an opportunity to practice and perfect your skills. Here are a few tips on how you can continue your development:

- Present at meetings in work

- Give workshops

- Deliver training

- Speak at local events

- Join toastmasters

- Give speeches at parties

- Say a few words at social events

- Present awards

These are just a few examples of how you can continue your journey. The important item to remember is to enjoy yourself. Look for opportunities to present in friendly environments in which you will be encouraged. As you master the skills move on to more challenging situations, bring your experience with you, and most of all apply the learning you have discovered on your journey.

Enjoy the success professional presentation will bring to you through competence and creditability.

Thank you,

Derek Fox
2010

Made in the USA
Charleston, SC
11 November 2011